Create Your Own
BONSAI

Create Your Own
BONSAI
With Everyday Garden Plants

PETER CHAN

WARD LOCK

Acknowledgments

I have long been aware of the need for a 'do-it-yourself' book on bonsai, and I hope this one will fit the bill. Writing this book has been great fun, especially since the designer, Colin Lewis, is also an accomplished bonsai grower. As always, I am indebted to my wife, Dawn, for her ideas for this book and for her help with the word processing.

This books is dedicated to my mother, who has always loved plants, and from whom I learned to love plants from a very early age.

First published in Great Britain in 1989 by Ward Lock Limited, Villiers House, 41-47 Strand, London WC2N 5JE

A Cassell Imprint

Reprinted 1991, 1992, 1993

British Library Cataloguing in Publication Data
Chan, Peter, 1940-
   Create your own Bonsai
   1. Bonsai. Cultivation
   I. Title
   635.9'772

ISBN 0-7063-6831-2

Printed in Spain
Photography: Chris Ridgers
Design: Colin Lewis Associates

Contents

PUBLISHER'S NOTE

Readers are requested to note that in order to make the text intelligible in both hemispheres, plant flowering times, etc. are generally described in terms of seasons, not months. The following table provides an approximate 'translation' of seasons into months for the two hemispheres.

NORTHERN HEMISPHERE				SOUTHERN HEMISPHERE
Mid-winter	=	January	=	Mid-summer
Late winter	=	February	=	Late summer
Early spring	=	March	=	Early autumn
Mid-spring	=	April	=	Mid-autumn
Late spring	=	May	=	Late autumn
Early summer	=	June	=	Early winter
Mid-summer	=	July	=	Mid-winter
Late summer	=	August	=	Late winter
Early autumn	=	September	=	Early spring
Mid-autumn	=	October	=	Mid-spring
Late autumn	=	November	=	Late spring
Early winter	=	December	=	Early summer

What is a bonsai?

A bonsai is a tree or plant grown in a container to resemble a full-grown tree on a miniature scale. However, simply growing a tree in a pot does not make it a bonsai. The tree and its container must together form a pleasing composition and should resemble as closely as possible the mature tree you would find growing in nature. A bonsai is essentially a beautiful thing: the miniaturization is only incidental.

All too often one sees little conifers and seedling trees planted in plastic trays or ceramic pots which are passed off as bonsai. Unfortunately these cannot really be called bonsai as they have no artistic character whatsoever. This is not to say that they have no long-term potential to become nice bonsai. However they would need to be worked on and refined before they could begin to be called artistic pot plants, which is what bonsai are. A bonsai must have an aesthetic quality about it, otherwise it will be no different from an ordinary nursery or garden centre plant. The scale must also be right. Thus it pays to find plants which have interesting trunks and small leaves since these will be more in keeping with the scale of the bonsai. They will also need some initial shaping and training in order to make them resemble more closely their full-grown counterparts in nature. Only in this way can the potential beauty of ordinary plants and shrubs be brought out to the full as bonsai. Most ordinary plants have potential for bonsai – some more so than others; the bonsai artist's job is to draw this out using all the various skills at his or her disposal.

What makes it dwarf?

A bonsai is not a naturally occurring dwarf species. Almost any tree or plant can be miniaturized for use as a bonsai. What makes a tree small is a combination of branch pruning and confinement in a container to restrict its growth. Just as a hedge would soon become unkempt and out of control unless pruned regularly once or twice a year, so a bonsai will become a mass and tangle of branches if its shoots are left to grow completely unchecked. Confining the roots in a container will restrict its vigour to a large extent and consequently the leaves and the spaces between leaves (the internodes) will become progressively smaller and tighter.

Does a bonsai have to be old to be nice?

Not all bonsai have to be old to be nice. A relatively young tree can be made to look very authentic and attractive by rudimentary shaping and pruning. It is a fallacy that all bonsai have to be old to be nice, and, increasingly, more and more people are beginning to recognize that a bonsai must first and foremost be beautiful in order to be appealing. Age, though important, is of less significance. There are some very ancient and beautiful bonsai in China and Japan which have been cared for over many generations and which as a result have incredible refinement. Not only are they very beautiful to look at, but the mere fact that they are so old commands a reverence all of its own.

Indoor or outdoor?

Bonsai are essentially outdoor trees because their natural environment is the open air. However, because of the increasing interest in indoor plants, certain mediterranean and tropical varieties of tree are being grown for use as 'indoor bonsai'. These are very similar to the plants sold by florists' shops and garden centres. Varieties include the small-leaved ficus, olive, pistachio, pomegranate and so on. You should however recognize that all indoor trees and plants benefit from being in the open during the warmer summer months because all plants love sunshine, fresh air and rain. Houseplants, and by the same token, indoor bonsai, benefit from being kept outside in the summer where their leaves are encouraged to become greener and their growth is 'tightened' by shortening of the internodal spaces, i.e. the spaces between each pair of leaves. A spell outdoors in the summer will do your indoor bonsai a world of good.

It is important to recognize the difference between indoor and outdoor bonsai as their growing conditions are quite different. Given the right care and attention indoor bonsai can be as interesting to grow as the traditional hardy outdoor varieties.

CHAPTER 1

Basic care of bonsai

A bonsai is a living plant and will therefore require regular care and attention. In some ways it is almost like a pet: it cannot be left for long periods without water, food and attention, but it is, of course, much easier to care for than a pet animal.

If you are given a bonsai as a present, all you need to do is to ensure that the tree is watered regularly so that it never dries out completely, and to remember to give it a little fertilizer from time to time. An occasional trimming of the growing shoots is perhaps all the basic care that is required. However, if you wish to create your own bonsai from various types of material, then it is important to understand some of the basic principles underlying the horticulture and aesthetics that combine together to make successful bonsai.

All bonsai are grown in a container of one kind or another. This can be a classic Japanese or Chinese bonsai pot, an improvized pot, or even a flat piece of slate. A bonsai should never be taken out of its container and planted in a garden flower bed as it would soon revert to an ordinary garden shrub or plant.

Bonsai pots come in many shapes and sizes. The size of pot is determined largely by the size of the tree that you wish to grow, and the shape is determined by the style and the general aesthetics of the bonsai in question. Put simply, the shape of the pot is dictated largely by one's aesthetic sense. If it looks right to you then it is probably right. All bonsai pots should have adequate drainage. This means that they must have large drainage holes. Some of the larger bonsai pots in fact have as many as six to ten holes. There is no need to make drainage holes on flat pieces of stone or slate because the water will simply run off.

Compost
The compost used for bonsai is essentially the same as any other good garden compost. Different bonsai growers have their own

When choosing a bonsai pot, make sure it has an adequate drainage hole and that there are no hollows on the bottom which would hold water. The small holes in the corners of this pot are for threading the wires through in order to hold the bonsai firm.

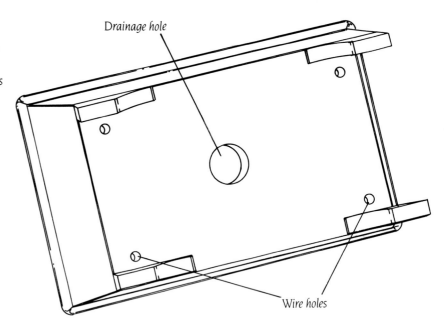

Drainage hole

Wire holes

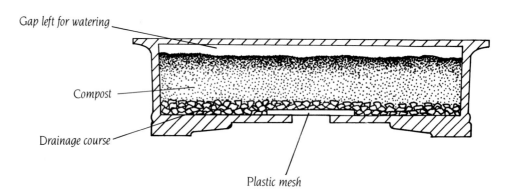

Gap left for watering

Compost

Drainage course

Plastic mesh

favourite formulae depending on the variety of tree they are growing. A general purpose compost such as a John Innes No. 2 is extremely good. There are specialist bonsai growers who use nothing but pure sharp sand for growing varieties such as juniper and pine, and certain types of indoor bonsai are now being grown almost exclusively in peat-based compost. A bonsai will come to no great harm so long as the compost is free draining and has adequate fertilizer from time to time. If in doubt just add a handful of grit or sharp sand to improve the drainage and you won't go far wrong.

Repotting

One of the greatest fallacies about bonsai is that you have to cut and trim the roots regularly, say once a year, in order to dwarf a tree. Of course nothing could be further from the truth and regular

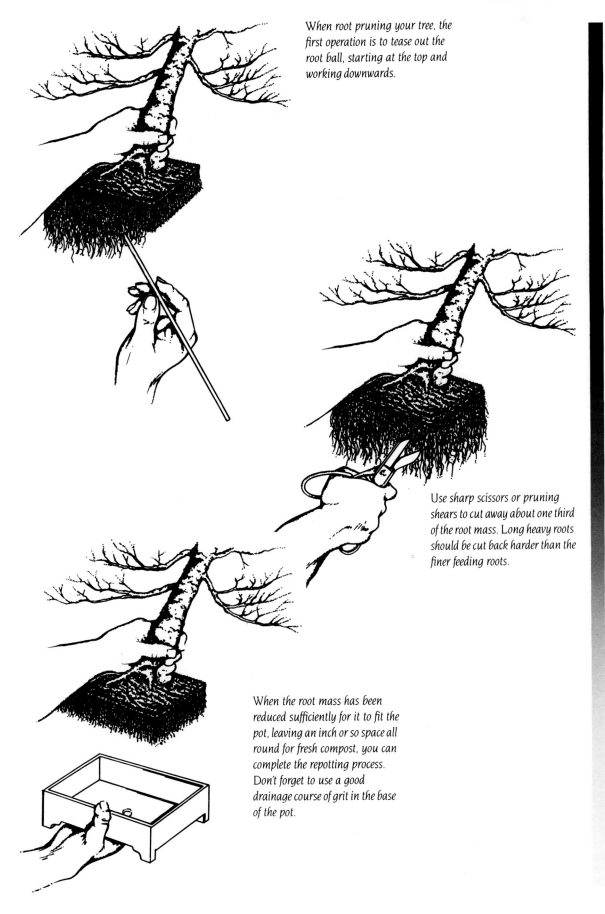

When root pruning your tree, the first operation is to tease out the root ball, starting at the top and working downwards.

Use sharp scissors or pruning shears to cut away about one third of the root mass. Long heavy roots should be cut back harder than the finer feeding roots.

When the root mass has been reduced sufficiently for it to fit the pot, leaving an inch or so space all round for fresh compost, you can complete the repotting process. Don't forget to use a good drainage course of grit in the base of the pot.

root pruning at such frequency could even be harmful. Bonsai are root pruned when they are pot bound so as to enable fresh soil to be introduced into the pot and to give the roots more space in which to grow. Never root prune a bonsai simply for the sake of doing so.

You should always take the tree out of the pot and examine the condition of its roots. If the tree is badly pot bound then it is perhaps time to root prune, otherwise simply put it back into its pot and let it grow on for another year. Root pruning is normally done at the beginning of the growing season, i.e. in early spring just before growth is about to start. Done at this time of the year the roots which have been freshly cut will not rot but will be able to put out new growth fairly quickly.

When repotting a tree, take away only sufficient root to enable the tree to be put back into its existing pot with some new soil. Once the tree has been repotted, it should be kept away from strong draughts and sheltered from any frost. The soil should be just moist but not soggy. Ideally the repotted tree should be placed in a cool greenhouse or in a coldframe. The watering should be increased as the new growth emerges. Do not fertilize a tree until it is well established, i.e. for deciduous varieties once all the leaves have fully opened and for evergreens when the tree is obviously putting out new green shoots. This is usually six or eight weeks after repotting.

Watering

Watering is one of the most essential aspects of bonsai. Surprisingly it is also one of the most difficult. During the growing season all bonsai will need to be watered regularly. It is not sufficient to rely on rainwater to supply the moisture requirements of your bonsai. During hot summer days you will need to water your trees once, if not twice, a day. The best time for watering is in the evening when the sun has gone down. On very hot days it is best to water before the sun starts to shine on the foliage.

To water a tree use either a watering can fitted with a fine rose, or an ordinary garden hose. You will need to drench your tree two or three times in order for the water to soak thoroughly through the soil. It is not sufficient simply to wet the foliage and the soil surface. If the pot has become really dry you may even need to immerse it completely in a bowl of water until the air bubbles stop rising, after which you should take it out of the bowl and let the excess water drain off.

Feeding

Feeding your bonsai is also an important part of care and maintenance. It is a fallacy to imagine that bonsai are starved in order to keep them small. A good bonsai is always in the peak of health. As with a garden plant or shrub, a bonsai will need to be fertilized regularly. This means applying liquid or granular fertilizer when the plant is growing so that it will get all the essential nutrients and trace elements which are essential to plant health. To do this you can use any of the proprietary plant fertilizers but at half their recommended strength. Feed a tree once a fortnight or even once a month. It is a good idea to set aside fixed dates for doing this so that you don't forget.

Placement

Traditional or hardy bonsai are kept out of doors and most people keep them on the patio near the house or alternatively near a window where they can be seen and enjoyed. A bonsai should not be exposed to the full sun all day long as this makes watering more of a problem. A suitable position is one where the bonsai will get sun for part of the day, i.e. either morning sun or afternoon sun. It depends very much on how your garden is positioned in relation to the house. Try to keep your tree away

If you have to keep your bonsai on a windowsill, it is advisable to secure it firmly by tying it on with wire or nylon string as shown.

Some indoor bonsai will tolerate or even prefer full sun but most will prefer to be placed where they receive good light but not direct sunlight. A table or shelf within three feet (1 metre) of a west-facing window would be ideal. Always check the natural habitat of your chosen species, this will give you a clue as to the best placement.

from draughts as these can cause quite a lot of damage to bonsai, especially in the winter. A sheltered position with sunshine available for part of the day is ideal.

Indoor bonsai of course require a little more thought and care in their placement. Certain varieties can stand direct sunshine while others are happier with light conditions but not direct sun. As a general rule most plants prefer to be in a light airy situation than in a dark corner which gets hardly any light at all. Of course the lack of natural light should not be a deterrent from growing indoor bonsai because there are artificial growing lamps which can be used to provide the light needed for plants to thrive. Indoor bonsai should not be placed on top of radiators or near fires as the leaves would soon get scorched. A window sill or the top of a dining table are suitable positions for indoor bonsai, provided there is sufficient light.

CHAPTER 2

Where to begin

Basic requirements

TOOLS AND POTS

Growing bonsai need not involve a vast outlay of money on pots and tools. There is a great deal of scope for improvization. Many everyday garden implements can be adapted for use as bonsai tools.

Perhaps the most essential tool for bonsai is a pair of sharp secateurs. Those which have the scissor action are better than the anvil type. Secateurs are used for pruning branches and bits of trunk which are not needed for bonsai. The other useful tool is a pair of ordinary household scissors. These are useful for root pruning and trimming shoots and twigs. A pair of wire snips can come in handy for cutting wire used for training the branches.

Proper bonsai pots can be expensive as they are usually high quality stoneware pots imported from Japan and China. If you

Pots come in many shapes and sizes, each suited to a different style or species. Shallow ones suit groups, while deep pots are best for cascades. Literati bonsai look good in round pots, and ovals combine well with elegant maples or zelkovas.

have facilities for making pots yourself, or know a friend who can make them, then this could be a very convenient, inexpensive source. However, the pots should be made of stoneware and modelled after classical bonsai pot designs.

Plastic bonsai pots are now becoming more easily available and are considerably cheaper than traditional stoneware pots. Small seed trays, such as the half and quarter size trays, are a good substitute for bonsai pots as they are the right shape and size. Plastic ice-cream or margarine tubs painted dark brown could also be used for training trees. Some bonsai enthusiasts make pots out of cement and concrete and these can be quite successful too. A nicely shaped piece of rock or slate could also be used as a substitute for a shallow pot. Forest and group plantings look particularly attractive when planted on slate.

COMPOST

As explained in Chapter 1 the compost is essentially the same as any other ordinary potting compost. The main requirement is good drainage and to ensure this, extra-coarse grit or sand should be added to give the compost a more open texture. A suitable compost which is fairly easily available is John Innes No. 2, which is basically a mixture of loam or garden soil, peat and sharp sand. You can buy this from most garden shops or make it yourself. You can substitute leaf mould for peat if you wish. Coarse building sand which has been left to weather in the open for some time is a good substitute for grit or horticultural sand. These are all very good ingredients for making bonsai compost.

Basic techniques

PRUNING

You must be prepared to prune in order to create bonsai. Much of the dwarfing process is achieved by pruning and the techniques used in bonsai are really no different from those for pruning ordinary garden shrubs and trees. Prune cleanly, avoid crossing branches and always prune to an outward pointing bud.

TRAINING WIRE

The wire for shaping the branches should be fairly pliable and for this reason copper or aluminium wire is generally used. Galvanized iron wire may be used but this is not ideal as it is too stiff to bend. Green plastic-coated garden wire is a reasonable substitute, but for most beginners copper wire from the inside of electric cables is probably as good as any of the wire used by the professionals.

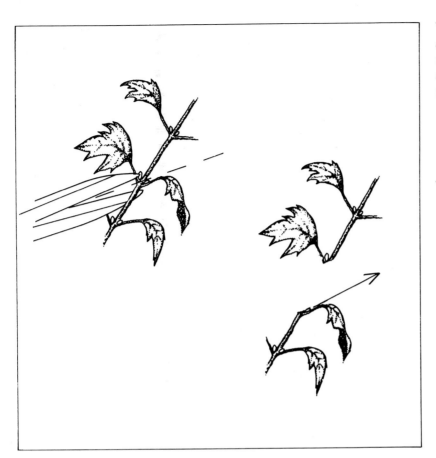

When pruning a bonsai
always try to prune to a bud
which is pointing in the
direction that the new growth
is required.

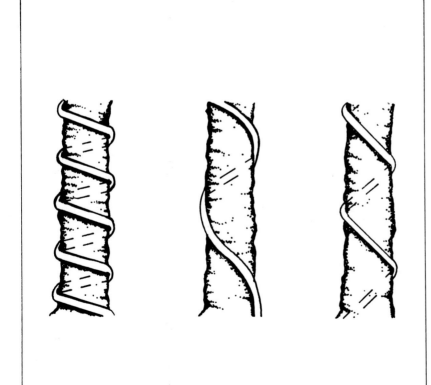

The wire on the left has been
applied too tightly and will
seriously disfigure the bark.

The wire in the centre has
been applied too loosely and
will have no holding power.

The wire on the right has
been applied correctly and
will hold the branch in the
desired position without
damaging the bark.

ROOT PRUNING

There are many who imagine that root pruning is what makes a bonsai dwarf. This is not entirely true. A bonsai should be root pruned only when it is pot bound – when the roots completely fill the pot – not as a matter of routine. The frequency of root pruning depends very much on the variety of tree. Certain varieties of tree are more vigorous than others. The more vigorous varieties may require repotting and root pruning once a year, although it is perhaps better to root prune once every other year if in doubt. Older bonsai which have reached maturity are root pruned much less frequently – say once every five to eight years.

The best time for repotting is in the early spring. If you have a conservatory or cold greenhouse, repotting may be done at any time between late autumn and early spring.

Root pruning is like cutting hair. Simply comb out the roots and snip off the long ends. By cutting off the excess roots this will encourage new and finer roots to develop. Do not cut off more than is absolutely necessary. As long as there is sufficient room for fresh compost to be introduced into the pot, this will do. An old table fork bent into the shape of a rake is ideal for teasing out the roots. Many tools can be improvized for the same purpose. A chopstick or hook is equally suitable.

CHAPTER 3

Bonsai styles

There are many different styles of bonsai which have been developed over the centuries. Although the definitions of these styles are quite precise they are only intended to be guidelines which should be interpreted by the individual bonsai grower to create an original and aesthetically pleasing result.

Some of the most common styles are illustrated below. Each style has been named but the definitions have not been included since the images should speak for themselves.

Chokkan – Formal upright style

Tachiki – Informal upright style

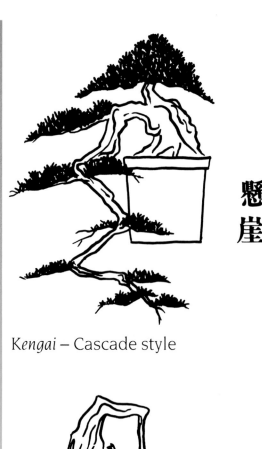

Kengai – Cascade style

Shakan – Slanting style

Neagari – Exposed-root style

Han-kengai – Semi-cascade style

Fukinagashi – Windswept style

雙樹

Sôju – Twin trunk style

株立

Kabudachi – Clump style

箒立

Hôkidachi – Broom style

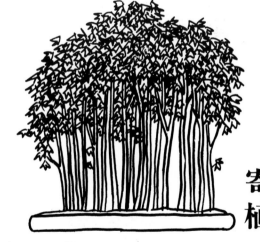

寄植

Yôse-ue – Group style

石上樹

Sekijôju – Root-over-rock style

CHAPTER 4

Growing bonsai from seed

There are many ways of creating bonsai. You can use ordinary trees and shrubs purchased from garden centres and nurseries or you can use plants taken from your own garden. Alternatively you can start from scratch by taking cuttings and raising seedlings. There are advantages and drawbacks to each of the different approaches, but perhaps the most challenging is raising bonsai from seed. Growing bonsai from seed is a relatively slow process, but it can also be the most satisfying. One of the main advantages of growing from seed is that you have complete control right from the very start.

Although raising bonsai from seed is a relatively slow process it is not as slow as one might imagine. Some very nice trees can be produced in as little as three or four years. It depends very much on how the trees are developed and trained. If seedlings are grown intensively they can attain quite thick trunks in a fairly short space of time. On the other hand if they are grown in small containers and never potted on, they will always remain very tiny. Creating a bonsai is in some respects like programming a computer. You can make it do almost anything you want it to.

Good quality seed is of course the key to success. If seeds are not viable to begin with, then no matter what you do, they will not germinate. The seeds should be purchased from a reputable dealer who can ensure that they have been stored properly or are relatively fresh.

Some seeds are easier to germinate than others. The easier varieties are usually those which do not require any pre-sowing treatment. Most hard-coated seeds from the temperate regions require this treatment in order to break the dormancy of the seed. Dormancy is nature's way of ensuring that a seed will germinate only in the spring when there is no longer any danger of frosts. If a seed were to germinate in the middle of winter, the frost would soon kill off the young plant. In nature the winter frosts help to rouse a seed from its sleep so that when spring comes it will germinate freely and grow on to become a strong young tree. Under controlled conditions the cold and frost can be reproduced by placing the seeds in a refrigerator or freezer. Either is suitable.

Seeds normally come sealed in paper packets or plastic bags. In order to stratify them, put them in a plastic bag with a small quantity of water. The seeds should be allowed to soak in this water overnight before being put into the freezer. Most seeds will benefit from being put into the freezer for about four weeks. After this period they can be taken out of the freezer and sown in the normal way in a mixture of peat and sand or ordinary seed sowing compost. You can either leave the seed tray on a kitchen window sill or put it in an airing cupboard for just three or four days to start the germination process. The seed tray should be covered with a plastic bag in order to conserve moisture.

Once the seeds show signs of growth, the bag should be opened gradually so as to introduce air into the environment. If the cover is not removed then seeds tend to get long and lanky and there is also danger of the seedlings 'damping off' from virus infection.

Some varieties of seed take much longer to germinate than others. Hornbeam, hawthorn and sometimes Japanese maple can take more than a season to germinate. If seeds do not emerge after two or three months, it is worth freezing the entire contents of the seed pan in a plastic bag for another three to four weeks. Repeat the germination process again in the hope that they might sprout. If this does not work, leave the seeds in the garden so that they can be stratified during the coming winter. There is always a chance that they will germinate the following spring.

When the seeds begin to sprout, remove the seed tray from the plastic bag and keep the compost moderately moist but not too wet. Never let the compost dry out completely. Overwatering and underwatering are equally damaging.

When the seedlings have put out two or three pairs of leaves this is the best time to pot them on into individual pots. Potting is best done in the early spring and may be continued up to mid-summer. If you have a greenhouse then you can continue to pot up right into late summer but no later than this. Seedlings are best potted up into individual two-to three-inch (5-7.5 cm) plastic pots to grow on strongly.

No shaping or trimming should be done during the first year. The seedlings should simply be grown on until they have sufficient vigour to withstand the training at a later stage. When the seedlings are well established in their individual pots (within two

There is no such thing as bonsai seed. The seeds used for bonsai are ordinary tree and shrub seeds. These are Chinese quince fruit (Chaenomeles lagenaria). The plants germinate very readily from seed. The ripe fruit can be collected in autumn and the seeds taken from inside and sown straightaway. Seeds sown in the autumn will germinate in about ten days, or they can be left until spring for spring sowing.

The seeds are best planted in small flowerpots or seed trays, using seed sowing compost or an equal mix of peat and fine silver sand. Quince and crab apple seeds germinate very readily and can be sown at any time of the year. When the young seedlings germinate they should be sheltered or over-wintered in a cold greenhouse or conservatory. Alternatively, simply place them on the kitchen window sill.

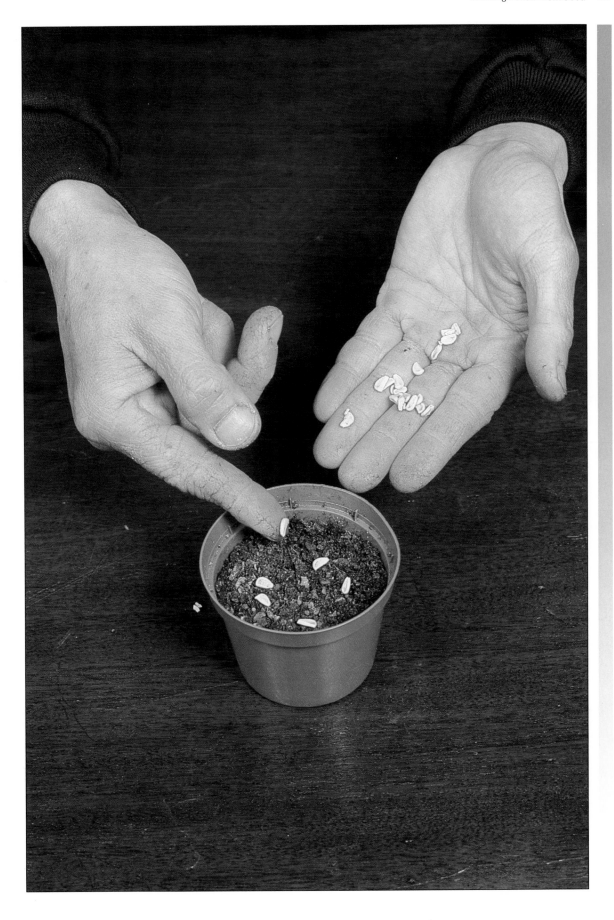

The young seedlings should not be pricked out until they have two pairs of leaves. Individual seedlings should be planted in three-inch (7.5 cm) flowerpots and grown on for a full year before any wiring or training is done.

Opposite: *This two-year-old seedling of Chinese quince was potted up into a three-inch (7.5 cm) flowerpot, and then into a five-inch (12.5 cm) pot for its second year's growth. It is about nine inches (23 cm) high.*

or three weeks they should be fed with a weak fertilizer to induce stronger growth.

In the second year the young seedlings can be shaped into bonsai. The roots should not be pruned at this stage as this will weaken the tree. You should decide fairly early on whether you wish to have a large bonsai or a smaller one. For a large bonsai, the seedlings should be progressively potted on into larger containers so that the tree will develop a fairly thick trunk. If you decide to keep a bonsai no more than three to four inches (7.5-10 cm high, the tree can be shaped into a tree of this size when it reaches a height of six to eight inches (15-20 cm) The extra height is to allow for pruning off the excess.

There are two basic ways of developing bonsai from seedlings. The first is the age-old Chinese method known as the clip and grow' method. This involves constant clipping and cutting back of the shoots until the desired shape is achieved. The second method is a more recent one using copper or aluminium wire for bending the tree into the appropriate shape. In the clip and grow method two-or three-year-old seedlings are allowed to grow strongly so that a moderate sized trunk is available. A seedling

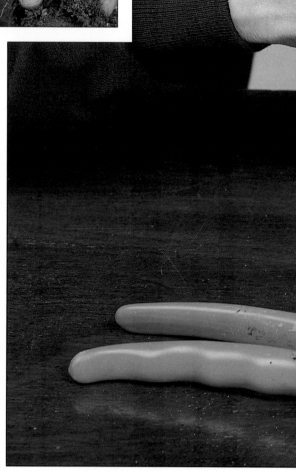

To promote bushiness, the tip or apex of the plant can be taken out and this will encourage the laterals to grow.

Even at this young age a healthy and vigorous plant will require root pruning if it is to fit a suitable bonsai pot. The most important thing to remember is to cut the thick tap roots hard back while leaving sufficient fine feeding roots to support the plant. The new, finer root system which develops will be reflected in a finer branch pattern.

can grow up to 12 inches (30 cm) high in a flower pot if grown well. Seeds grown in open seed beds can sometimes attain a height of two to three feet (60-90 cm) in the first couple of years. Japanese maples and zelkovas can grow three to four feet (90-120 cm) in the same period. However since the objective is not to grow trees which are too tall, they should be cut back at regular intervals so that all the goodness is channelled into the trunk. In the clip and grow method, branches which are growing in the wrong direction are removed so that the leading shoot can be encouraged to grow in the desired direction. In this way the tree can be made to grow in any direction or shape.

Pruning is usually done in the spring and summer but not later than the late summer. In spring, shoots which have developed in the previous year are cut back to half their original length or to one or two nodes of the previous season's growth.

The modern method of making bonsai by wiring is much simpler and quicker than the ancient clip and grow practice. A seedling of about two years old can be wired, but anything younger is not really suitable as it will not have developed sufficient trunk thickness to withstand the bending with wire.

The most basic shape used in bonsai is what is known as the informal upright or 'S' shape. In order to bend the trunk, wind a piece of wire of the appropriate thickness from the base of the trunk all the way up to the apex. This can be done with either aluminium or copper wire. The wire should be wound on fairly tightly; if it is too loose it will not have much effect. Once the tree is wired it can be bent into the desired shape. The wire should be left on for a complete growing season during which time it will set in the form in which it is trained. If the wire appears to be biting into the bark or trunk it should be removed and wired in a slightly different position so as to avoid disfiguring the bark.

The plants are about ⅛ inch (3 mm) in diameter and they can now be wired to give the trunk a more interesting shape. Once the tree is wired into shape and planted in the appropriate bonsai pot the little seedlings take on a completely different character. By wiring the trunk into an 'S' shape the height of the seedling is reduced to give a more squat appearance.

CHAPTER 5

Growing bonsai from cuttings

For most gardeners taking cuttings is one of the most satisfying activities. Growing a plant from a cutting has the added bonus of getting something for free. I can still remember the thrill I experienced when I struck my first maple cutting. Not many years ago maples were considered to be exotic plants and it was generally believed that they could not be propagated from cuttings. You can imagine my delight therefore when most of the cuttings I took actually produced roots in just two weeks! I was to learn later that many species which are considered difficult to root are not so difficult after all.

Some plants are, of course, easier to strike from cuttings than others, while certain varieties do not strike however hard you try. One learns by experimentation. To add to the confusion, there are softwood cuttings and hardwood cuttings. Some cuttings are taken in the early part of the growing season and others in late summer or early autumn. It is therefore important to know which variety lends itself to a particular kind of treatment. Building on the knowledge of others can save a lot of time and effort.

Creating a bonsai from a cutting has many advantages. Apart from the fact that it is free, you also have the satisfaction of seeing your bonsai grow from scratch. Many famous and important bonsai masterpieces in Japan have been developed in this way and there is of course no reason why you should not be able to make a masterpiece bonsai yourself by this method. As with growing from seed, growing bonsai from cuttings need not necessarily be a long process. Very nice looking trees can be produced in as little as three or four years.

Certain species of plant propagate more easily than others from cuttings. Forsythia and viburnum are two good examples. A branch or twig pushed into the ground will root in a matter of weeks, but there are certain processes which help to provide ideal conditions for the cutting to root. First, to ensure that the leaves do not lose too much moisture the cutting should be kept in a closed environment such as a clear plastic bag or a propagating frame. Of course professional growers go to great lengths to provide these ideal conditions. They use polythene tunnels and propagating benches with sophisticated automatic misting equipment. For most amateurs this is not within reach, nor really necessary. All that is needed is a plastic seed tray or flowerpot, some peat and sharp sand and a clear plastic bag. A heated propagator with soil warming cables to provide 'bottom heat' can be a great help as this can speed up the rooting process, but you can still achieve a fairly high success rate without such equipment. Not all plants like bottom heat. In fact conifer cuttings are best propagated without, since the heat can dry up the cuttings too rapidly.

There are two types of cutting – softwood and hardwood. A softwood cutting is taken in early or mid-summer using shoots which have been produced earlier in the spring. The ideal time to take such a cutting is when the stem is just beginning to turn woody. A hardwood cutting on the other hand is taken in late summer or early autumn, when the shoot has actually hardened and ripened.

Softwood cuttings may be taken with or without a 'heel'. A heel cutting is one that has been torn from the stem of the plant and has a bit of the bark of the stem still attached to it. A 'nodal' cutting is one that has simply been cut off just below a leaf joint. You can use either a pair of sharp scissors or a scalpel blade for this purpose.

Most deciduous trees and shrubs, such as the Japanese maple, trident maple, pomegranate, elm, cotoneaster and willow, root easily from softwood cuttings. However not all varieties of plant can be propagated from cuttings and it is only by trial and error that you will get to know which varieties can be propagated by this method.

The ideal softwood cutting is one which is about three to four inches (7–10 cm) long and with no more than two pairs of leaves. The soft growing tip where the leaves have not yet formed should be pinched out as it often wilts and dies anyway. Pinching out the growing tip also encourages a bushy plant to develop when the cutting produces roots. Softwood cuttings may be taken with or without a heel. When the cuttings have taken they will need plenty of light to stimulate the production of new leaves and roots, but they should be shaded from direct sunlight as this can cause the leaves to wilt and scorch. When a cutting has 'struck', new shoots will be seen to grow from the leaf joints. A gentle tug at the

Most junipers propagate very readily from cuttings. Heel cuttings root faster than nodal cuttings. To make a heel cutting tear off a shoot of about four to five inches (10–12.5 cm) from the main trunk or branch of an established tree. The end should be trimmed with a pair of sharp secateurs or a knife and then dipped into hormone rooting powder. The cutting should be inserted into a seed tray or five-inch (12.5 cm) flowerpot filled with pure peat or with an equal mixture of peat and sharp sand. The cuttings can take from between one and three months to root.

Once the cuttings have rooted, they should be potted up into individual flowerpots and grown on for a full season.

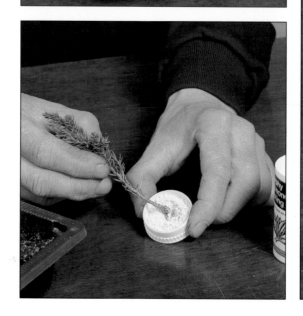

A strong bushy plant can be developed in just one year. The training and wiring should be done in the following year. By simply wiring the trunk into an 'S' shape, a bonsai in the informal upright style is created.

When planted in a bonsai pot this two-year-old cutting is quite presentable. Over the next couple of years the crown and foliage pads can be developed, and this will give the tree a more mature look.

cutting will soon tell you if the roots have formed. If the cutting comes away easily then the chances are that there are no roots. If the cutting holds the soil firmly then roots will have formed.

The ideal medium for rooting cuttings is either pure sphagnum moss peat or an equal mixture of moss peat and sharp sand. Softwood cuttings are best taken in a deep seed tray or five-inch (12.5 cm) flowerpot. Hardwood cuttings can also be struck in deep pots but are better struck in the open ground.

Once the cutting has rooted it can be taken out, potted up into individual three-inch (7.5 cm) flowerpots and grown on. It should be grown vigorously for a full year before any training or wiring is contemplated. The training is no different from that which you would give to a plant from a nursery or garden centre – after all, most nursery plants have been raised in the same way. The only difference is that you have grown this yourself.

CHAPTER 6

Bonsai from garden centre plants

The increasing popularity of gardening means that garden centres are becoming more widespread. As a result plants and shrubs are more easily available today. Many of the plants sold in garden centres are suitable for bonsai. All that is needed is guidance on the choice of variety and what to look·for in each individual specimen.

There are three guiding principles to remember when choosing plants for bonsai. The plants themselves must have interesting shapes, the leaves must be fairly small and the trunks fairly thick. All three attributes help to give your potential bonsai that instant aged look. The trunk is perhaps the most important aspect of any bonsai because it is this which makes your shrub look like a real tree. An interesting trunk shape is therefore vital because this cannot easily be altered. The shape of the branches is not such a problem because the branches can be rearranged by wiring.

Most nurseries and garden centres today tend to be very conscious of their presentation, and the condition of the foliage of their plants is therefore of the utmost importance. The trunks and branches are secondary. Thus, very often those plants which have been scorched by the sun or damaged by frost will have untidy leaves and these are put to one side and sold off as seconds. This invariably applies to old stock which has been lying around for a year or more. Such plants are of course ideal for making into bonsai because they are much older to begin with and their trunks will normally be much thicker than the new plants that have just come into the garden centre as new stock. The condition of the leaves should not worry you because these can be grown again. A rummage around the 'seconds' area is usually extremely worthwhile and can be a rich source of potential bonsai raw material.

The examples in this chapter are intended to give you some idea of the possibilities which exist in your local garden centre today. The raw material is there in plenty. All that is required is a little courage and imagination. Bonsai is really quite easy. There is no mystique about it. The subjects chosen for this chapter were all from garden centres and the step-by-step photographs show how they were transformed with just a little bit of work.

Potentilla fruticosa

Potentilla

Potentilla is not often seen as bonsai because it is not a species that one would imagine could be used for this purpose. However, potentilla make excellent bonsai for two reasons – they have lovely trunks and beautiful flowers. This is also a species that is easily available in nurseries and garden centres.

Potentilla are hardy, vigorous shrubs. When planted in the garden they can spread to about four feet (1.2 m) in diameter. Their trunks thicken in time giving them a tree-like appearance. They can be pruned fairly rigorously, without sacrificing many of the flowers. In recent years, many hybrids of this species have been developed; their flowers range from red to pure white, with several shades of yellow in between. However, my favourite is still the pale yellow variety, *Potentilla fruticosa*.

What to look for

Being shrubs, potentilla tend to be multi-stemmed rather than single-stemmed. But this in itself is not a disadvantage; on the contrary, multi-trunked specimens can be used for making into any of the multiple-trunk styles such as twin, triple, five and seven trunk etc. Try to find plants that have interestingly shaped trunks as these will form the basic structure of your bonsai. If branches are not in the right place, new ones can be encouraged to grow over the next couple of seasons.

Special points

Potentilla are such vigorous shrubs that they soon become a tangle of twigs and branches when left in the sales beds of garden centres for any length of time. Consequently this is a plant which is often sold off cheaply when it becomes old and straggly. This is ideal bonsai material as the trunks will be much thicker and older. Do not be too concerned if the plant is pot bound as the roots can be disentangled when you repot the tree. Potentilla can be used for making into most of the traditional bonsai styles.

This potentilla was bought from a garden centre in late summer when the old stock was being sold off very cheaply. The plants had remained unsold for over two years and had become straggly and overgrown. This particular plant had in fact rooted itself into the display bed. However this was ideal material for bonsai. The trunk was gnarled, old and twisted, but the plant was otherwise generally healthy. It was also covered in beautiful yellow flowers. I chose this particular specimen because the trunk had an interesting shape and there were lots of branches to choose from for making it into any of the recognized bonsai styles

With a bushy plant such as this, the first thing to do is to thin out some of the branches. The long straggly shoots are cut back to within 12 inches (30 cm) of the main trunk. In making any bonsai from ordinary garden centre material, it is not unusual to remove at least half of the existing branches. The remaining branches usually provide more than enough choice to form the basic structure of the tree. The aim at this stage is to remove the long straggly shoots, so as to reveal as much of the main trunk as possible. Showing the trunk is very important because it is only by making the trunk visible that the plant begins to look like a tree.

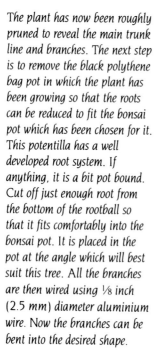

The plant has now been roughly pruned to reveal the main trunk line and branches. The next step is to remove the black polythene bag pot in which the plant has been growing so that the roots can be reduced to fit the bonsai pot which has been chosen for it. This potentilla has a well developed root system. If anything, it is a bit pot bound. Cut off just enough root from the bottom of the rootball so that it fits comfortably into the bonsai pot. It is placed in the pot at the angle which will best suit this tree. All the branches are then wired using ⅛ inch (2.5 mm) diameter aluminium wire. Now the branches can be bent into the desired shape.

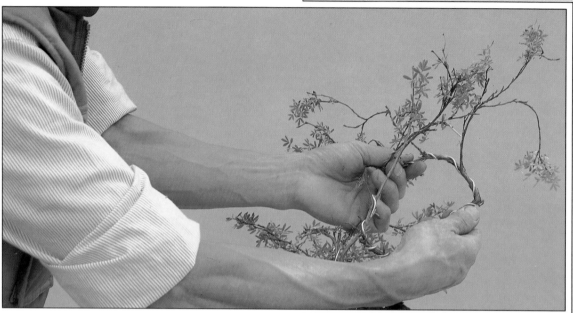

Once the branches have been wired it is quite easy to bend them in the direction in which you wish them to lean. I decided to make this potentilla into a semi-cascade style because it had a nice side branch which would hang very elegantly as the main cascading branch, leaving the other branch to be used as the crown or apex. This bonsai was created in late autumn when it was fairly safe to tease and cut the roots. The branches used for the design had a few flower buds left on them and the warmth of the late autumn sunshine brought them out into blossom a fortnight later. The blue pot was deliberately chosen to complement the pale sulphur-yellow flowers.

Pyracantha angustifolia

Pyracantha

The pyracantha or 'firethorn' is often seen as a hedging or wall shrub. It is a lovely plant with many good qualities: it is evergreen, it has creamy-white flowers in spring, followed by bright red berries in autumn. Although it is extremely vigorous when grown as a garden plant, it is not entirely hardy when grown as a bonsai. Pyracantha needs winter protection. Apart from this however the plant is very suitable for training into bonsai. It is used quite extensively in Japan for this purpose. Most garden centres stock pyracantha and there are many new varieties that have orange, yellow and even pink berries.

What to look for
Always look for plants that have interesting trunk shapes. A bent or gnarled trunk is more interesting than one that is absolutely straight. Good low branches are preferable to a few high ones. A few dead branches here and there do not matter as new ones will soon grow again.

Special points
Pyracantha has long sharp thorns so care is needed in handling this plant. The older branches can be slightly brittle which means that they cannot be bent too much. Of course the younger branches are more pliable and these are better suited for wiring into the desired shape. The young shoots of pyracantha are prone to attack by greenfly and the plant is also susceptible to soft scale. These pests are not a problem and most insecticides can deal adequately with them.

This pyracantha may not look very exciting to the average gardener. It has a few dead branches, the trunk is kinked and it is rather pot bound. But for the bonsai enthusiast this is good raw material. The white roots indicate vigour and health and the kink in the trunk is not a disadvantage; on the contrary it gives the plant added interest. A closer look at the trunk just below the soil level reveals a good spreading root system going down a further couple of inches (5 cm). The soil can be removed to this level giving the trunk an extra couple of inches (5 cm) in height.

To get this massive root-ball to
fit into a bonsai pot, some of the
surplus roots will need to be cut
off. The roots are first teased out
so that we can judge how much
to remove. Cut off just enough
root, leaving about an inch
(2.5 cm) of space all round the
perimeter of the pot. Next, place
some small pieces of plastic mesh
to cover the drainage holes. Put
the tree back into the pot and fill
it up with soil, making sure that
there are no air spaces between
the roots. You can check this by
pushing your fingers into the
compost and pressing firmly. If
there are large gaps, your
fingers will penetrate easily – in
which case more compost will
need to be added.

Once the tree is potted the next step is to trim the branches to give a pleasing overall shape. The aim is to create a conical outline. Cut off the tips of the long protruding shoots. Spread out the branches so that you can get a better idea of the eventual shape of the tree you wish to create.

Now wire the trunk and the branches. This is done with soft aluminium wire. The thickness of the wire will depend very much on the thickness of the trunk or branch to be bent. Here we have used ⅛ inch (2.5 mm) diameter wire. Always use one piece of wire to link two adjacent branches. As a rough guide the length of the wire should be about one-third longer than the combined lengths of the two adjacent branches. The wire should be wrapped around the branches fairly tightly. Start by wiring the branches at the bottom first and then work your way towards the apex of the tree. You may wire in either a clockwise or an anti-clockwise direction. It does not really matter which way you do it. The wiring should be kept neat and the front of the tree should

be left uncluttered as far as possible. Do not criss-cross the wires as this will look untidy.

Once the branches have been wired they can be bent into virtually any shape you want. The branches are bent so that they lie horizontally or hang slightly downwards.

The overall shape to aim for is a broad- based triangle. The branches are also spread evenly around the trunk, with more branches at the rear than at the front. Adjacent branches should not overhang each other as this will exclude light and could cause the lower branches to die. After just a few minutes work this is the result you can obtain: A pleasing looking tree from what was once a tangle of unruly branches. Notice that the front of the tree is kept fairly open. The overall shape is triangular and the branches are fairly evenly distributed along the length of the trunk. The branches start from a third of the way up the trunk.

Picea abies 'Gregoryana'

Dwarf spruce

This is really a dwarf conifer of the spruce family. It is very slow growing and has a lovely rounded shape. It is best used for bonsai when it is no more than nine inches (23 cm) high. Even small cuttings of this plant make very attractive miniature bonsai. It puts out new growth in spring which is a lovely bright green colour. Not many spruces are suitable for bonsai. Those that are suitable are *Picea glauca* 'Albertiana conica' (dwarf Alberta spruce), *Picea abies* 'Little Gem', and of course the famous 'Ezo spruce' *Picea glehnii*. The ordinary Christmas tree *Picea abies* or Norway spruce is too coarse for use as bonsai, as are most of the remaining spruces. Many of these have whorls of branches which make them very difficult to use for classic bonsai shapes.

What to look for

Look for shrubs that have interesting trunks. This may mean parting the foliage or removing dead foliage from inside the tree and closely examining the base of the trunk. Some of the dwarf spruces have multiple trunks which make them highly suitable for multi-trunk bonsai. The needles should be green and healthy and not sickly yellow. A lot of plump young buds is usually a sign of vigour. It does not matter if the tree is a bit pot bound as the roots can always be teased out and pruned.

Special points

As this is a dwarf variety of spruce, even fairly small plants can be quite old. Most dwarf spruces will therefore have interesting and gnarled-looking trunks. Do not worry if the foliage is a bit sparse inside the shrub as new foliage can be made to grow again with careful pinching back of the older shoots. Look for branches in the right position, especially the first and second branches which will form the basic structure of the bonsai. Spruces attract red spider and this can cause the needles to drop. Red spider and other insect pests can be controlled with most proprietary insecticides.

Opposite Picea glehnii, *similar in many respects to the more common but more compact* Picea abies *'Gregoriana'.*

This dwarf spruce seems an unlikely candidate for bonsai. It is simply a rounded mass of foliage. The plant itself is fairly vigorous as can be seen from the large root-ball. The fleshy brown roots almost completely fill the pot.

A closer examination of the plant reveals that there is more potential than first meets the eye. There are in fact two trunks joined together at the base. Both trunks have immense character and this would make the plant very suitable for training in the twin-trunk style. There are also more than enough branches for developing on.

The very compact root-ball can be considerably reduced to fit the fairly shallow bonsai pot.

The roots are teased out and the root-ball is then placed roughly in position in the bonsai pot in which it is to be planted. Cut off just enough root for the root-ball to fit snugly into the bonsai pot. Leave about an inch (2.5 cm) of space all round the perimeter. About two-thirds of the root-ball will need to be removed, but this will not harm the tree in any way. New roots will soon grow and these will be much finer than the ones that have been cut off.

When the root-ball has been reduced suffiently the tree can be potted into a bonsai pot. The soil used is the standard bonsai mix, or John Innes No. 2 with extra grit added. The tree is planted so that both trunks are fully visible from the viewing side. The next step is to cut away the superfluous branches in order to give the shrub a more tree-like appearance. The branches are arranged in flat tiers with the help of wire.

Aluminium wire of 1 mm in diameter has been used as this is perfectly adequate for the fine branches of this tree.

By revealing the trunk and creating more space between the branches this dwarf spruce has been made to look like a tall elegant pine tree. In bonsai it is quite usual to use one species to create the image of another species. This is a good example of what can be done.

Rose

Most gardeners will know that the rose comes in many guises. There are the hybrid teas, rugosas, old-fashioned shrub roses and so on. However only those varieties that have small leaves and flowers are suitable for bonsai. Anything else would look out of scale. This makes the miniature roses an obvious choice. But there are also varieties that have naturally small leaves and flowers, such as 'ballerina' and 'nozomi'. These small-leaved varieties are excellent for growing from seed as they remain small for a very long time. Growing rose bonsai from seed is in fact much better than using material that has been grafted, since the graft union is not very elegant.

What to look for

Try to use varieties that are fairly disease resistant. Nothing could be more unsightly than a rose bonsai that has black spot or mildew. Although these diseases can be treated they tend to persist. When selecting roses for bonsai from garden centres look for ones that are well grafted. The graft union can sometimes be used to great advantage if it has a lot of character, as in the example shown in this book.

Special points

Roses and most flowering trees when grown as bonsai prefer a loam-based compost. Flowering bonsai should therefore be potted in John Innes No. 2. They will need to be fed regularly during the growing season. Any flowering or fruiting fertilizer such as rose or tomato fertilizer is very good for this purpose.

This shrub rose was purchased from a garden centre in the late autumn. It was taken out of the black plastic pot straightaway and the roots cut to fit the small cascade bonsai container. The thick roots of the root stock were deliberately left high and exposed in order to give the potential bonsai an older and more gnarled appearance. Where the graft was lumpy and ugly the shoots and much of the wood in that area were cut away. The long branches were then roughly wired with aluminium wire to create a cascading effect. One or two of the upright branches were left in place to form the crown of the tree. In the coming spring this, tree should be covered in delicate pink blossom. An unusual bonsai created from very ordinary garden centre material.

Juniperus chinensis 'San Jose'

Chinese juniper

'San Jose' juniper is a low-growing ground cover shrub. It is normally sold as a plant suitable for camouflaging manhole covers in the garden. It is a vigorous grower and can spread to eight feet (2.4 m) in diameter in about 15 years. This juniper is suitable for bonsai as it can stand very cold winters on the one hand and very hot, dry summers on the other. Although it does not mind being positioned in the sun all day, it does turn slightly yellow in these conditions. However any good general fertilizer should soon turn it green again. The San Jose juniper has prickly foliage, but this is a small price to pay when the shrub has so many other good qualities.

What to look for
Most junipers have interesting trunks and branches but the San Jose juniper beats them all. When choosing a plant from your garden centre, look for one that has a fairly thick trunk at the base and one that is preferably gnarled and twisted at root level. It does not matter if the foliage is a bit ragged and untidy because the foliage will soon grow again with care and attention. Make sure that you choose a plant that has many low-growing branches as these will be needed for forming the lower structure of your bonsai.

Special points
Junipers are one of the best species for bonsai. They look good and the scale of their foliage is right for the tree. They have very interesting trunk shapes and they are extremely hardy. As a rule, junipers do not require any winter protection in temperate climates. They are not usually attacked by pests, but are slightly prone to scale insect infestation. Juniper scale is a small flat creature which is no more than $1/16$ inch (1 mm) in diameter and greyish-white in colour. Most proprietary brands of insecticide will soon get rid of this pest.

A nice bushy plant with a great
deal of potential for bonsai. A
closer look reveals a lovely
curving trunk which is fairly
thick at the base. The bark has
interesting colour and texture
too, all of which adds to the
character of this tree. Although
the trunk is about an inch
(2.5 cm) in diameter at the base
it is still fairly pliable and can
be bent into the right shape by
using the appropriate gauge of
wire.

In order to bend the trunk of this tree a fairly thick gauge wire will need to be used. We have chosen 4 mm diameter wire in this case. The wire is inserted into the soil close to the trunk to anchor it firmly. It is then wrapped tightly round the trunk and coiled all the way up to the apex. Once the trunk has been wired it can be bent into an 'S' shape. A suitable bonsai pot can now be chosen and the roots teased out gently in preparation for potting.

Once the tree is potted up the branches can be wired. A thinner gauge of wire 1.5 mm is used for the branches as these are not as thick as the trunk. Always use one piece of wire for two adjacent branches. Every branch should be wired in order to give the tree a precise shape.

View the tree from the front and at eye level to position each branch correctly. About three quarters of the foliage of this tree has been pruned off, leaving only the choicest branches for the final composition.

The final trimming is a manicuring process in which all the little twigs and shoots which were not wired are removed. Shoots which hang downwards from each of the branches are also tidied up. Final touches include the placing of pieces of moss on the soil surface to make the tree look as if it has been growing in that pot for a long time. The finished tree is a simple elegant design. The branches from inside the main curve have been removed so that the sweep of the curve is enhanced. This bonsai is reminiscent of the 'literati' style as the lines are very clean and the tree itself looks like a Chinese brush stroke painting.

CHAPTER 7

Bonsai from your own garden

It is not often realized that bonsai are in fact ordinary plants despite their exotic appearance. Many still believe that they are some special botanical species. When I first became interested in bonsai in the late 1960s bonsai were extremely difficult to obtain and, needless to say, very expensive too. I decided to create my own bonsai tree by copying examples in Japanese and Chinese bonsai picture books and by using shrubs and small trees from my own garden. The experience has proved invaluable over the years and I have derived immense pleasure from it.

The average garden is a gold mine as far as raw material for bonsai is concerned. Almost any plant, shrub or tree can be dug up and made into an instant bonsai, not to mention the hundreds of cuttings and layerings which can be taken from stock plants.

Garden plants suitable for bonsai include the common ash, azalea, beech, berberis, box, camellia, cedar, flowering cherry, cotoneaster, crab apple, cypress, elm, ginkgo, hawthorn, hornbeam, holly, juniper, larch, English field maple, Japanese maple, oak, pine, privet, pyracantha, quince, rhododendron, spruce, sycamore, willow, wisteria and yew. This list is by no means comprehensive. I am sure the reader can think of many others that I have omitted to mention.

The first step in the bonsai process is to dig the plant up and get it to a large container or pot so that it can get accustomed to being planted in a container. The next step is to prune the shrub roughly into a triangular shape by thinning out some of the branches. If the plant has sufficient root the training and shaping can be done immediately. If the tree is not showing signs of vigour then it is perhaps better to wait until it is growing properly before any training is attempted. As long as the plant has sufficient root and the root ball can be made to fit into a bonsai pot the chances of survival are very good indeed. If the plant does not have sufficient root or is not sufficiently vigorous then you will need to be patient and wait until the plant is well established. Bonsai does require some patience and to wait a year is not too much to ask.

Prunus subhirtella 'Autumnalis Rosea'

Winter flowering cherry

Flowering trees are always a great joy, especially if they bloom early, and the winter flowering cherry is perhaps the earliest of them all. It flowers from late autumn right through to mid-spring. The lovely delicate blossom is like little stars that shine through the grey haze of winter. It is an ideal subject for bonsai as the flowers are so petite.

Most of the other flowering cherries can in fact be grown in pots and are therefore suitable subjects for bonsai.

What to look for

Flowering trees such as cherries, crab apples, peaches, apricots and wisteria are usually grafted in order to induce flowering from an early age. If the same trees were grown from seed they could take anything from 10 to 12 years before beginning to flower. However grafting has its disadvantages because the graft union can sometimes be very ugly. When looking for potential material for bonsai, try to find a tree that has a neat graft, i.e. one that is smooth and blends in with the rest of the trunk. For bonsai work it is best to use trees that are grafted very low – almost at root level. Bush trees will of course be better suited for bonsai than half standard or standard trees as they will have branches that are much lower down.

Special Points

Fruiting and flowering trees can be potted into bonsai pots from late autumn to early spring. If the potting is done in autumn then some winter protection is necessary. For established trees already developed as bonsai, repotting is best done in late autumn as repotting in early spring can cause the flowerbuds to drop.

This winter flowering cherry has been in training for only four years. It was made from a large eight-foot (2.4 m) high standard tree which I dug up from my garden. The roots were reduced in two stages. When I first dug up this tree it was potted in a large wooden box. Two years later it was transferred to this bonsai pot which I made specially for it. All the branches and the new leader have been grown since training was started. When the tree is in bloom it is magnificent.

This is a young winter flowering cherry which I planted in a shrub border two years ago. The tree was purchased as a bush — hence the low branches. The graft can hardly be seen and the root system is very compact. A tree of this size would make an ideal bonsai.

The long straggly branches have been removed leaving a fairly compact shrub about three feet (90 cm) high. Most of the branches are concentrated at the top which makes this a difficult subject to convert into a smaller bonsai. There are two options: either cut off the top 12 inches (30 cm) to encourage new branches to grow; or leave the tree largely as it is and create a taller bonsai using most of the existing branches.

I decided to use most of the existing branches of this tree so that the finished example would be more immediately recognizable as a bonsai. The thicker branches are removed, leaving behind the fine branches which are more in keeping with the rest of the tree. Most deciduous shrubs produce new branches very readily and it should not be too long before new growth begins to sprout from lower down the trunk. If I had opted for the longer term solution, i.e. cutting the tree down to about one foot (30 cm) in height, a complete set of new branches would soon have developed. This could take as little as two years to achieve.

Some wiring is necessary to give the tree a more pleasing shape. At present all the branches spring upwards, which is the natural tendency of most juvenile trees. But for bonsai it is better to encourage the branches to hang downwards, which gives the tree a much older appearance. Wiring down the branches also encourages more lateral branches to develop, thus inducing flowering shoots. Fruit tree growers practise the same principle with apple and pear trees. They peg down the branches with string to prevent them growing straight up, and this encourages more fruiting and flowering buds to form. Notice where the thicker branches have been removed. The cuts are made flush to the trunk.

Once the branches are wired and shaped the tree can be potted up in a bonsai container. A fairly deep bonsai pot would be better, as flowering trees prefer to have a deeper root run. A blue pot is chosen as this will contrast with the lovely pink flowers. The tips of the roots are cut off so that the root-ball can fit the bonsai pot. It is not necessary to remove all the garden soil from the root-ball, although some of it should be replaced with good bonsai compost. Make sure that the soil fills the pot completely and that there are no air spaces between the roots. Press in the soil firmly with the fingers to ensure good contact between the compost and the roots. After potting, the tree should be watered lightly and kept in a sheltered position for a couple of weeks.

Juniper communis `hornibrookii`

Common juniper

This variety of juniper is widely used as a rockery plant because of its cascading habit. It is not a fast grower but can attain a spread of about five feet (1.5 m) in ten years. As it creeps along the ground it sends out roots from the branches that touch the soil, thereby layering itself. Like all junipers this variety is extremely hardy. The foliage is a lovely bright green with a silvery sheen. Because of its prostrate habit, the hornibrookii is well suited to the cascade style. Junipers are not fussy about the type of soil they grow in. They are equally happy in peat or chalky soil, but the soil must be free draining.

What to look for

Try to find a plant that has a reasonable sized trunk with lots of twists and bends. Branches are not a problem with this variety as there are usually more than enough to choose from. Look for a reasonable sized plant – something between nine and 15 inches (23–38 cm) long. Anything larger might be too big for a beginner to handle. Bigger trees would also require much bigger bonsai pots, which are quite expensive to buy.

Special points

This juniper has prickly foliage but is very distinctive as it resembles the needles of the Japanese white pine with the white line down the centre of the needles. When grown as a bonsai it is quite vigorous and constant pinching is necessary in order to keep it in good shape. Juniper grows best in free draining compost. Extra grit should be added to the compost to enhance drainage. Regular feeding will also help to keep the foliage in good colour.

Opposite Juniperus rigida *'yatsubusa', similar in most respects to the more* common Juniperus communis *'hornibrookii'.*

This juniper was planted in the garden only a year ago. During that time the tree has almost doubled in size. Notice how vigorous the roots and branches are. This plant would make an excellent bonsai because it has a lot of branches and a very interesting overall shape.

Before deciding on the style, examine the plant carefully. Look at the way the branches are placed in relation to the trunk and assess the length and character of each branch. Start by teasing out the root-ball and then trim away any weak and straggly branches which have no use in bonsai composition.

This juniper has two strong branches growing from very near the base of the trunk. One of these could easily be bent downwards to form the main branch of a cascade-style tree. The two principal branches are wired using 3.5 mm diameter aluminium wire. Take care not to trap any of the small branches in the wiring process. Once the branch has been wired it can be bent into any shape. Bend the longer of the two branches downwards to form the cascade. The shorter branch can be wired upwards to form the crown.

The tree is planted in a tall cascade pot as the additional height is needed for this style of bonsai. Note how the branch zigzags all the way down. This creates movement and interest. Some of the smaller lateral branches are pruned away to show the very interesting line of the cascading branch. The crown still needs to be shaped and this will be done next.

The apex of the tree is far too dense. Some of the branches need to be thinned out. About a quarter of the top can be removed and what remains can then be wired into the shape of a small bonsai. The finished tree is simple and elegant – quite a change from the tangled mass of branches with which we started out.

Cotoneaster horizontalis

Cotoneaster

There are many varieties of cotoneaster. Some are ground cover plants with tiny leaves, while others grow into large trees. The variety most commonly found in gardens is the herringbone or rock cotoneaster – *Cotoneaster horizontalis*. This is a medium-sized shrub that grows vigorously in almost any type of soil. It can often be found growing in paving or in the cracks of walls. It flowers profusely and is a great favourite with the bees. The flowers are followed by red berries which last well into the winter. As a bonsai subject it is perhaps one of the most versatile since it can be trained into almost any of the recognised bonsai styles.

What to look for
With garden material you can use plants of any size for bonsai. I have made bonsai from cotoneaster that have had trunks of two to three inches (5–7.5 cm) diameter. These were potted into large pots and are now beautiful specimen trees. For most beginners, something about half an inch (2.5 cm) in diameter would be ideal. Cotoneasters are also very good for small bonsai. Young seedlings and cuttings can be trained in minute pots for mame bonsai. Look for plants that have interesting twists and bends to the trunk. Do not worry if the plant in the ground is too large as the branches can always be cut back and new branches will soon grow again.

Special points
The cotoneaster is not a fussy plant. It can grow under the most arduous conditions. I have seen cotoneasters growing in the cracks of walls with almost no soil at all. This makes them highly suitable for growing in the root-over-rock style. The long roots are draped over a nice piece of rock and the ends planted in the soil of the bonsai pot. When planted in this way, the tree will give the appearance of an aged tree growing on a hill top or out of a rocky cliff. Its very prolific branching habit enables the bonsai artist to select almost any branch that is required for styling the tree.

This cotoneaster has been dug up from the shrub border in the early spring. It was planted as a one-year-old seedling three years ago. The plant is therefore only four years old. This is an example of how rapidly some seedlings can grow in a relatively short space of time. It is just the right shape and size for a medium sized bonsai. A cream coloured oval pot is chosen as this will complement the red berries very well.

The tree is placed roughly in position in the oval pot and the long protruding roots are cut off. As the root-ball is fairly compact there is more than enough root left to support the tree.

The tree is then potted up, planted in precisely the same angle as it was growing in the ground. Very little shaping has been done so far. The only branches that have been removed are the long straggly ones which were three to four feet (90–120 cm) long. The double trunk is retained as this is an interesting feature and would make a good twin-trunk style bonsai.

It would be very tempting to leave all the branches and berries and simply trim the ends to make a nice rounded shape. However this would not be in the long-term interest of the tree as a bonsai.

In bonsai one has to visualize how the tree will develop in the future. It is therefore very important to get right the structure at the outset. The object now should be to create a pleasing basic framework around which all the future branches and foliage pads will hang. Cotoneasters are very vigorous shrubs and many new branches and shoots will sprout from the trunk during the coming season. These can be selected and trained on, to form the final shape of the tree.

CHAPTER 8

Tray landscapes

Tray landscapes and forest plantings have universal appeal. Their popularity stems from the fact that they look so natural. It is said that a well made forest planting can be so convincing that you could almost imagine yourself walking in a real forest. There is peace, tranquility and beauty and this can be enjoyed over a long period of time because the plants are living.

These lovely compositions are not as difficult to make as you would imagine. They require the minimum of skill and just a little imagination.

Tray or miniature landscapes have their origins in China where this art has been practised for over 2,000 years. It is all part and parcel of Chinese garden art, in which miniaturization plays a central role. Tray landscapes are to the Chinese what rock gardens are to the English gardener. The only difference being that the Chinese miniature landscapes are true to scale and intended to represent natural scenery in three dimensional form. Rock gardens by contrast are created mainly for the interest of the plants themselves. Scale is not so important. There is also an analogy with landscape painting where the artist captures on a piece of canvas or paper the essence and mood of what he sees in nature. The bonsai artist of course does this with living plant material.

Tray landscapes are still made today in China and Japan. In fact the Chinese refer to bonsai as *Penjing* or 'potted scenery' because their trees are usually planted with rocks and miniature ornaments to create the right perspective and scale. Some Chinese potted landscapes consist almost entirely of rock. The rocks in this case symbolize mountains and are often displayed in very ornate bonsai pots or marble stands.

The Japanese tray landscapes are more natural in appearance. They resemble more closely what is actually seen in nature. Volumes can be written about this very interesting subject – but in a limited guide such as this, it is not possible to go into depth. The object here is to give you a feel for what this aspect of bonsai entails and to encourage you to have a go at making it yourself.

In creating a tray or miniature landscape, the aim is to make a picture, not simply to put a few plants together on a tray. The composition must have an aesthetic appeal. Some people have a natural gift for arranging things tastefully. They seem to have a perfect sense of balance and harmony. But this can also be achieved with practice. There is of course nothing to stop you copying the ideas of others and improving on them. Practice makes perfect and in the fullness of time you could make lovely miniature landscapes yourself. The example that follows will give you some idea of what is possible using very ordinary plant material that can be purchased in almost any garden centre or nursery.

The material chosen for this
tray landscape consists of five
little Chamaecyparis
elwoodii *cuttings, two
miniature alpine rhododendrons*
(Rhodendron impeditum)
*and a pot of alpine grass of the
acorus family. A large flat piece
of grey Welsh slate measuring
about two feet (60 cm) long is
used as the pot or base. The
slate not only looks nice but is
fairly cheap and easy to obtain.
A stoneware bonsai pot of
similiar dimensions would be
very expensive.*

The first step in making any tray landscape is to arrange the plant material in different positions in order to find the most pleasing overall arrangement. The best solution will always stand out because it is immediately recognizable Similarly a bad arrangement will tell you that something is not quite right.

Here we have grouped together the five elwoodii cuttings on the left hand side to make a tight cohesive unit. The two little rhododendrons are placed on the right to form another separate clump. The two groupings are linked together by the slate and soil which will be filled in later. The acorus is split up into three portions to form separate little clumps.

Once the plants are in position, soil is placed in a mound on the slate to hold them all in place. Loamy garden soil is best for this as it is sticky and can hold the plants together well. If ordinary potting compost is used this will be washed away with the first shower of rain. Notice how the plants are arranged at different heights to give added interest. The soil is mounded up in two places to give the impression of two small hills with a valley between.

The soil can now be pressed
down firmly and smeared on to
the slate to hold the entire
composition together. The heavy
clay soil also retains moisture
better than ordinary compost
and will therefore make the job
of watering the tray landscape
that much easier.

When all the soil has been
firmly pressed into position
pieces of moss can be added to
give the planting a more mature
look. The best moss to use is
that which grows on paving. This
can be scraped off with a flat
scraper or garden trowel and
laid on the mounded soil to look
as if it had been growing there
for a long time.

CHAPTER 9

Fun bonsai

I have called this chapter 'Fun bonsai' because there is enormous pleasure to be derived from making and growing plants which, though not strictly bonsai, have a very strong bonsai flavour to them. There are certain plants which are neither trees nor shrubs but which nevertheless make interesting 'pseudo bonsai' and bonsai accessories. Plants such as ferns, grasses, herbs, cacti and succulents, have interesting colours, textures and shapes and offer the bonsai enthusiast tremendous scope for creativity and improvization.

These plants should be on the small side, preferably no bigger than nine to 12 inches (23–30 cm). They can be used on their own as single specimen plants or planted in mixed groups. Unlike traditional bonsai which can live for decades or even centuries, fun bonsai are not intended to be long-lived subjects. A few years is as much as one can expect from them. Because the object of bonsai is to create a picture with living plant material, it is not strictly necessary to use actual trees and shrubs in every case. Compositions using grasses, ferns and herbs make delightful miniature landscapes. In bonsai, plant arrangements of this kind are called 'accent plantings' and they are normally used in conjunction with the larger trees when displayed at exhibitions. Their purpose is to act as a foil to counter balance the grandeur of the large traditional bonsai. The plants most often used for accent plantings are grasses, dwarf bamboos, small flowering alpines and dwarf herbaceous plants. Young plants of certain ferns and hostas make particularly nice 'accents'. Some of the more unusual New Zealand grasses are also very suitable. Carex and houtinyas are good plants to use.

Accent plantings are usually grown and displayed in bonsai pots. The pots may be deep or shallow depending on whether a single plant or a mixed group of plants is used.

Certain herbs and succulents which have a tree-like appearance can be grown to look like traditional bonsai. They can be shaped by pruning into most of the traditional bonsai styles. Rosemary, thyme, wormwood and most of the crassulas are very suitable subjects for this kind of treatment.

In China there is a tradition for growing chrysanthemums in bonsai pots. They are shaped like bonsai and are grown mainly for their beautiful flowers in autumn and winter. All the training is done in just six or nine months from cuttings. After the flowers have finished the plants are pruned back to their stumps and the chrysanthemum stools are used for propagating next year's plants.

In Japan, accent plants are seasonal. They are only displayed at certain times of the year when they look their best. Thus plants grown for their spring flowers are displayed in spring and those which are grown for their autumn colours will be displayed in autumn, and so on. In this way, there is constant change and variety throughout the year. The Japanese have great empathy with nature and this is very much in keeping with Japanese tradition in which even their flower arrangements reflect the changing seasons.

The pictures that follow are intended to give you some idea of the range of fun bonsai that can be made with non-traditional bonsai material. This might be anathema to the bonsai purist – but for ordinary gardeners it is really great fun! I have always maintained that in bonsai it is the end result which matters – how this is achieved is not important. After all, bonsai is an illusion.

Some of the woody silver leaf herbaceous plants make nice accent plantings and fun bonsai. This is wormwood which can grow up to four feet (120 cm) in diameter in the herbaceous border. This plant however has never grown higher than six inches (15 cm) over the last two years. It flowers profusely each summer but is best kept as a foliage plant as the flowers are rather straggly.

By constant pinching of the growing tips the new leaves are always bright and fresh. The woody stem gives it a very tree-like appearance.

The common crassula, or jade plant, makes a nice indoor bonsai. It is very easy to keep as indoor bonsai because it thrives in dry, warm conditions. In fact it looks better when kept on the dry side as its internodes (distance between each pair of leaves) are close and compact. It also has thick stems which resemble tree trunks.

By simply putting the crassula into a bonsai pot, the appearance is immediately altered. The shape of a bonsai pot can have quite a dramatic effect on a tree. The rectangular pot here is more suited to this tree. Some training of the branches is necessary in order to improve the overall shape. As with traditional bonsai, each tree has a front and a back. The front or viewing side of this tree is shown opposite. This enables you to appreciate the twin-trunk shape.

The cycad (Cycas revoluta) makes a lovely fun bonsai for indoors. The palm-like leaves and woody stem have a tropical flavour. They are well suited to growing in pots. As with most indoor bonsai this particular plant likes to be grown out of doors in a shady position during the summer.

Sedums are very popular plants for growing as accents. They look particularly handsome when grown in little bonsai pots or when grown in little clumps at the base of larger bonsai trees. When grown in little bonsai pots, they are used to complement the larger trees.

Bamboos make interesting bonsai subjects. The dwarf varieties are particularly suitable for growing in small pots. The taller plant in this picture is the variety popularly known as 'Buddha's belly' because of the waisted shape of the stems. The composition on the right is an accent planting that was made five years ago for my display at the Chelsea Flower Show. It is still growing very strongly although it has never been repotted.

Index